WITH ALL THY GETTING, GET THYSELF TOGETHER FIRST

TANEKA THORNTON

Taneka Thornton

Copyright 2019 Taneka Thornton

All rights reserved. No part of this publication may be reproduced, distributed, or transmitted in any form or by any means, including photocopying, recording, or other electronic, mechanical methods, without the prior written permission of the publisher, except in the case of brief quotations embodied in critical reviews and certain other noncommercial uses permitted by copyright law. Any references to historical events, real people, or real places are used based on the author's remembrance. Names, characters, and places are products of the author's remembrance.

Front Cover Image by Beyond The Book Media LLC

Book Design by Beyond The Book Media LLC

CONTENTS

Introduction   v

1. Living my best life (So I thought)   1
2. Change Is Good   13
3. GO   26
4. Healing in the Go   39
5. Leaving it all behind   50
6. The Finale   55

Acknowledgments   71

INTRODUCTION

Picture it. Gastonia, 2017. I am waiting at the courthouse just before 9:00 am so that my soon to be husband and I can get our marriage license. This all seems so surreal to me. I can't even describe what I am feeling at this point. This day had finally arrived, and I will be marrying the man God chose for me later today. I have such peace of mind even though we are marrying only after knowing each other for 19 days. How could this be? Who does things like this?

Getting to this place was not an easy task. I had to do things that I do not want to do. I had to let go of people, places, and things to get to this level of faith. Clearly, nobody told me that the road would be easy, but I truly believed he did not bring me this far to leave me. Sometimes I look at my husband, and I am amazed that I was blessed with so much favor to receive such a gift. I could not have done this if I had not gotten myself together first. I tried so many times to get to this place but wasn't successful because I was doing it out of self and what I thought I wanted. God knew what I needed to get me to this level and beyond. This would require me to go from works to faith. I don't take what he has done lightly, but I share it with you so that you can know what it means to get thyself together while obtaining things.

Chapter One
LIVING MY BEST LIFE (SO I THOUGHT)

January 2011 was going to be a different year for me. I was determined to find love, and I was going to make it work no matter what. I had no luck in this department, but I knew what I had to give. I was a good cook, a nicely shaped body, kids were well mannered, I had a job, and I was the type of woman a man would want. I had my own house, and I was holding it down. I could not believe that I was still single, and nobody was interested in me. This cannot be the life I was meant to live because I had so much to offer. I remember going to my cousin Tiffany's house, and we started drinking some wine (from a box). It was cold and good going down, and I was just excited to be there and not at home. I looked down at my hands and noticed a small bump between my ring finger and index finger. It was itching, but I kept on drinking. I thought it could have been the wine because Tiffany later told me that it had been in the refrigerator for a while.

Nevertheless, I proceeded with my drink and my two steps. Later in the week, I discovered more and more bumps were popping up. I work with children in the daycare, and something is always going around in there, so I just thought I caught something from one of the children. No big deal until it began to cover both hands. I had black spots all over them, and this was not just another case of the heebie-jeebies. I show up to work, and my coworkers thought I had scabies and suggested that I go to the doctor to make sure, and they should be able to prescribe something. Once I went to the doctor, they referred me to a dermatologist because they could not figure out what was going on with me. At this point, I am starting to get concerned because this was messing up my plan of finding a boo. Nobody wants to be with someone who has a skin disease and has some flaws. I needed to present perfection if I am going to land the man of my dreams. It became difficult to hide the spots, and there were days I did not leave my house, other than to go to work. I was becoming frustrated because I did not have an answer. I was beginning to worry and ask what is wrong with me?

The dermatologist prescribed creams, but they didn't work. I felt so isolated because not many people knew what I was experiencing, but being a homebody was nothing new for me. My house was the party house, and everyone came over there. During this time, interaction was limited. I went on as usual, and one night I fell asleep. Nothing was abnormal about this night until I woke up the next morning. My life, at that point, would never be the same.

IT'S TIME TO DIE

All my life, I have been what you would call a dreamer. I can dream about things, and eventually, it would come true. I always paid close attention to them because they would be so real that I thought it would be happening at that moment. I have dreamed of car accidents, and they came to pass. I have dreamed of drive-by shootings, hidden agendas, and my family's favorite one would be the pregnancy dreams. Anytime I dreamed of being pregnant, someone close to me or their friends would be pregnant. I take dreams seriously.

One night in the early spring, I dreamed I was in the car with a close friend and three others in the back. We were having a good time riding on the highway, listening to music, and just enjoying ourselves. As we were driving, my friend Tonya looked at me and said it is time for you to die. Now mind you, I am looking at her like what did you say. Tonya repeated it. It is time for you to die. At that moment, the three people riding in the back disappear one by one. At this point, it was only her and I who remained in the car.

I am sitting there stunned because I wasn't sure if Tonya was for real or if she was joking. I face forward, and when I look back over to the left, Tonya is gone. I am riding on the highway with no driver and no idea of where I am going. It's as if everyone I knew was gone, and I was left all alone. The next thing I know, I am walking down a dirt road. I have never been this way before, so it is not a familiar road to me. As I begin to look to the left and the right, everyone that I had ever dated or been in a relationship with is standing on both sides. It felt like a soul train line, and it's my turn to go down. They are reaching out for me and trying to grab me, and I was walking past them as if I am trying to get away. I knew I didn't want to stop and interact with any of them because I had been there and done that. I wasn't trying to go there again. After the last one's attempt was unsuccessful, they all disappear. I am now on a paved road, and I can see my children sitting on a curb. The boys are lined up according to their age, and my daughter is last. I don't say anything to them, and when I got to my daughter, I said, whatever they tell you to do, do it. I repeated it as if she is not paying attention or understanding the words that are coming out of my mouth. After saying it twice, I get up from her and turn around, and I say, *I surrender*. After releasing those words, a bright light shot out from a statue and lit up the entire sky. Then I woke up.

The only thing I could do was cry. I was so traumatized that I could not get myself together. I could feel the dream. I was not ready for that dream, and I did not know what to do with the information. I could not wait until morning because I needed to share this with my mom. I knew she would know what to do with it. I don't know what time it was, but I got up and called her immediately. I could not tell her without crying because it was so real to me. I was sobbing and snotting and could barely get the words out. All she said to me was you need to get yourself together and get where he says you need to be. Uh, is that all you have for me? Can't you see that I am traumatized? I want you to tell me that it probably doesn't have any meaning, but deep down in my heart, I knew better. I knew he was getting a message to me. He had already shown me beforehand that he speaks to me in my dreams, so I could not back out that easily. I understood that change needed to come because either I was about to die physically or needed to die spiritually; either way, there must be a death.

It didn't take long for me to decide that I had to move. Where I grew up was not the place that I was going to mature at. It was hard trying to live a life that was pleasing to God and be in the same company that I shared so much with. There had to be a separation. I had no choice. I felt like Abram when God told him to get from the land of his father. He had to move out to understand what God had in store for him. I wasn't sure where he was taking me, but I knew I had to leave to find out. It was hard to leave in the beginning. This was all that I had known for 32 years. I was born and raised here. My children's families lived here. Even though I am moving to a place where my mom had resided for about 11 years, I still had no connections to that place. This would be new for not only me but the children as well. I would be taking them from their familiar place to a place unknown. No matter what, I was not about to risk it. So, I told the children that we were leaving. At first, they did not understand why we had to leave, but they were excited. This was about their future as well, and what affects me affects them. We must be willing to go through it together. I have always been a person who was up for a challenge, so I was anticipating the change. I began to pack, and that's when I realized how much stuff I had accumulated over the years. I could not take it all with me, so I started giving stuff away. I did not want to have a yard sale because I did not have time to waste on something that I really did not see beneficial for me.

I had parties where people would come and look in my closets and whatever they wanted they could have. I was not about to be pressed or stressed over stuff. If the Lord takes it away, he can give it back. It didn't take long for me to clean out my house. I was leaving a four-bedroom house on section 8 to live in a two-bedroom apartment with my mom and four children. Talk about sacrifice. None of that bothered me because I knew it had to be done. It took me 23 years to move out of my parents' home, and here I am, after 9 years of being on my own, going back to the beginning. Sometimes you must go back to go forward.

MY NEW PLACE

Rome, Georgia, was not the place I wanted to live ever. I had visited often during my summer vacations or for the holidays, but I did not want to plant my roots there. When I first started visiting back in 2001, it was a small town that looked like nothing good was going on there. I wasn't impressed at all, and the men there was not something I wanted, so moving there was not an option. God has a way of getting you to a place that is for your betterment and not your entertainment. I officially became a Georgia peach on July 10, 2011. I was overwhelmed, but glad I made the transition. I needed a fresh start without the reminders of the things that did not work, relationships that did not last, or the hearts that I had broken. I was in a new city, and nobody knew me. I was on an even playing field.

I probably could find that man I was looking for, and I would be able to present my best foot forward without any of the baggage. So, for now, it's all good. I made a decision that since I was in a new city, I was going to change careers. I would work in fast food, customer service, anything other than childcare. I was burned out and ready for a change. I had kids and didn't want to spend another day with someone else's. I was searching all over the place for jobs, and I could not find anything. I was headstrong about doing my own thing, not knowing that God had a whole purpose for this move. I tried my best to stay in my own lane, and nothing else mattered. I was able to get the kids into school. My oldest son, Taye, was in the band back home, and he wanted to be in the band down here.

Being that this is a football state and they are big on the bands, they were already practicing and had assigned out the percussion parts. Taye could join the band but would need to play a different instrument. He agreed, but the band director saw him playing around with the other students. The band director told him that if he could learn the piece over the weekend and perform it for them, he would be able to move into the percussionist position. Taye accepted the challenge. He went home and started on it immediately. Come Monday morning, Taye was ready to show them what he was made of. After he finished, he received the permanent spot in the percussion. Not only was I benefiting from the move, but my children were as well. Look at God. Won't he do it?

The next few weeks were becoming a challenge because I still had no luck in finding a job outside of childcare. I was trying too hard to get away from that that I did not realize I was holding up my own blessings. I finally gave in and put in three applications. The first two I did not feel good about because when I walked in the place, the atmosphere was not so welcoming. I did not have anybody to check with about who was hiring at the time, so my mom was the one who told me about the last daycare center. I went in and got the application and filled it out quickly. I had no more time to lose, and I needed God to open the door without hesitation. The lady called me for an interview, and once I got there, it was nothing ordinary about it. The director asked me a few questions and then offered me the job. She told me she knew she was going to hire me from the first time she met me. This was just protocol because of the policy in place. I had no idea how easy it would be to walk in what was for me because I was too busy being about my own business. I am so relieved that I did not allow that opportunity to pass me by.

RESISTING THE GRAVITY PULL

After landing the job, I felt like I was headed in the right direction. I had a place to stay, a job, and the kids were adjusting quite well. If this is what God had for me, I can dig it. I was getting comfortable, and I wanted to continue to live my best life in this new city. I connected with some neighbors that my cousin told me about while he lived here. They were cool, and they would become my drinking partners. My mom asked me what my intentions were, and I made it very clear that I still smoke cigarettes and weed, drank alcohol, and I wasn't about to stop for anyone right now. Being that my mom is a pastor, she had a way of inquiring about my salvation without asking me directly. I was flexing my grown muscles.

I wanted her to know that I didn't come back to her house as a child. I am an adult with children, and what I chose to do with my time is my business. After saying all of that, I knew that was not what I was supposed to be doing. I could feel God walking behind me, calling my name. He would reach out to me, and I would intentionally go the opposite way. I was not ready yet. I am living the life that I wanted, and no one was going to stop me from doing that (so I thought). I fought hard to suppress what I was feeling. I would go to church, and any time the spirit of God would begin to move, I would slip out and go to the bathroom. I did not want to let go and let God in those services. I was not crying or singing until the spirit fell upon me. I did not want to participate.

I would stay home, especially if I knew what church they would be attending because I knew the spirit would be high in that place, and I didn't feel like getting high. Why am I fighting to stay alive when I already know he said it was time to die? I am not going with the flow, and I know it. This continues from about September until December 31, 2011. On New Year's Eve, I did not want to attend watch night service; neither did I want to go out and party. I was at a crossroads, and I could not decide which way I wanted to go. My mom did not pressure me to go to church, but I could tell she knew something was up. I was becoming fed up with not being able to be free. I felt trapped and stuck within myself. Something had to give, and it had to give ASAP!

THE DAY I DIED

Happy New Year. It is now 2012, and here I am looking for something amazing to happen. This time around, I am tired. I am sick and tired of being sick and tired. I am tired of the hurt and the pain that I am causing myself. At this point, I don't want a man or anything of that sort. I want a brand-new life to go along with the move I made 6 months prior. I was done. I got up early, thinking I don't want to continue to smoke cigarettes anymore. I wanted to be free of alcohol and promiscuity. I needed to be delivered from this. I was lying on the floor, just tired. I reached over and grabbed my cigarettes, and I only had two left. I let out a sigh because I didn't want to smoke them, but you can't just *not* smoke them, that's a smoker law. I mustered up the strength to go outside, and I light up one. I planned to smoke one and then later smoke the other one. Anyone who smokes knows that you never give away your last cigarette. You can give one away and keep the last one for yourself. I don't know who made that up, but it is true. Ask any smoker, and they will tell you the same thing. I am standing outside, hating the fact that I am smoking, and I really want to stop. By that time, my neighbor comes outside and ask me if I had a cigarette. I said yes immediately and handed him the cigarette. I put out the one I was smoking and walked back in the house. At that moment, I felt free. I knew something happened because I didn't want to do it anymore. It's as if something came and took it away from me, and I was finally free from that bondage. I could now look myself in the mirror and be proud of the person I was looking at.

Back in December, a tornado came through and tore up the

building I was working in, so I was out of work for a few extra days. We were not sure when we would get back inside the building, but a part of me was ready to get back now that I am smoke-free. It was Wednesday, January 4, and I was home alone. The kids were back in school, and my mom was at work. I could no longer fight back the tears. On that day in my living room, I surrendered to Christ. I cried out to him to come into my life. I was tired of running. I was tired of dodging those feelings that kept coming over me. I was tired of being sick and tired. I was tired of chasing after relationships only to eventually end up losing them. I was ready to turn around to the one person who continued to pursue me. Who never gave up on me and who thought I was worth it.

I could no longer deny him access to my heart. I opened it that day, and I opened it wide. I was ready, and he knew it. Before long, I received a phone call from my cousin Marsha. I could not wait to tell someone the good news, and she called just in time. I had to make a confession that Jesus was Lord over my life, and I was glad that he was in my heart. Marsha was so happy for me, and she knew that it was real. I had not been so sure of a thing in my entire life until this moment. You never know how it would hit you, but when it does, the evidence of a life change is immediate. After I got off the phone with her, it rang again. This time it was my boss asking if I wanted to work at the other facility until our building was finished. I told her yes without any hesitation. I was ready to get back to work now that I have the man I always wanted and who genuinely wanted me.

WHAT I LEARNED

There comes the point in your life where you must decide what you want. I spent many years looking after people and their feelings, wants, and desires and neglecting mine. I wanted more for my life as well as my children's life. God knows what and who we need, and when it is time for you to fulfill the purpose of your life, he will let you know by any means necessary. Sometimes you must leave that place of familiar to get to the favor that he has for you. I did not see myself moving away. I wanted to become established in my birthplace. The bible says in John 3 that you must be born again. Death must take place to bring forth life. Unless a grain of wheat falls to the ground, it cannot bear fruit. In other words, it must die in order to produce. Getting me together first allowed me to place my children in the position to receive. Your move is not only for yourself but for those who are with you or who will come behind you and follow. You must be willing to break out of fear and move into what God has ordained for you. If you can leave behind the noise and move into the mountain for your greater, you will be able to rise above any situation that you may face. God truly has your best interest at heart. I know you think what you have going on is what's best. Believe me, it is nothing compared to what is to come from your obedience to him. He is not out to harm you but to help you to be all that he created you to be. Don't continue to run from him. He is not going anywhere, and you will feel so much better once you let go and allow him full reign in your life. He will not fail you.

Chapter Two
CHANGE IS GOOD

If any man be in Christ, he is a new creature. This is how I felt after receiving him into my life. Being pursued by someone who is ready to give you everything was new for me. I was ready and eager to face anything that was thrown my way. I wanted to know as much as I could about him, and I wanted those around me to experience him like I had. I was reading the word day in and day out. I had my bible with me at work, and instead of taking a smoke break, I would pull out the word and read. I was head over heels in love with him, and I needed to know as much about him as I could. I had a zeal for him, and I wanted to be with him all the time. I would get off from work and have bible study with my mom. I had finally found a relationship that was benefiting both of us. What had I been doing with my life before this? I can't believe it took me this long to surrender to someone who wanted me. This felt right, and I did not want it to end.

Before accepting Christ into my heart, I made a vow to myself that I would not allow another man to touch me sexually until I got married. I was tired of the pointless sex that I was getting from the guys I was dating. I needed something that meant something to both of us and not to just get laid. I realized that only I could change it, and I owed it to myself to at least try. Being that my now relationship was more spiritual than physical, I had no problems staying focused. I could not see him, but that did not matter. I was used to hearing from guys and not really seeing them, anyway. I was good, and nothing was going to take my focus away from him. The more time we spent together, he began to reveal some things to me. Christ started showing me things like ministering and preaching the word. No matter where I would turn, I would see those words. I tried to push it out of my mind as if I am hallucinating things, but it kept coming before me. Eventually, I asked my mom what it meant, and she said the message seems clear to me. Go forth and do what he is calling you to do. That was a big step to take since I just received him into my life just a short while ago. I was thinking Christ is moving a little too fast because I still had an idea of what I wanted to do. I felt like I was saved now. I could date and find the man of my dreams. I know I am not going to offer up my body, so what harm was it to get the man first and then say yes to God. He understands right? Little did I know it does not work like that.

MAN OR MINISTRY

Working at the daycare, I was able to meet people without having to search for them. Every two weeks, we had a delivery guy come in and deliver supplies for us. The first guy, Bill, was ok, but then he stopped coming. Next thing I know, we have this dark chocolate coming in and bringing the deliveries. I was head over heels for this guy. Chris wore a brown uniform, and I just knew he was the best thing next to sliced bread. I would watch him from a distance and hope he would notice me and start a conversation. It appeared Chris would not do that, so I decided to make the first move. I got up the nerve to speak one day, and he turned and smiled at me. I thought I was going to lose it. For the next several months, we played a smile at each other or wave game. I did not want to do that forever, so I made up my mind to be more direct.

Meanwhile, Christ is trying to get me to accept the calling that is on my life. I wanted to say yes, but I knew if I did, I could not have the nice piece of dark chocolate, so I ignored him. I acted as if Christ was not talking to me. I was determined to go forth with my plan.

So I got up one day, and I put on an outfit that would turn heads and did my hair so I would look up to par. I was going to ask Chris if he had a girlfriend and if not, what was the possibility of us getting together. He came in, and I asked was he seeing someone, and he said yes, I am. Chris proceeded to tell me that if he were not in one, he would have asked me out a long time ago. So here I am again feeling rejected and like a fool for falling for someone who is not available. I held off accepting my calling because of some guy. I felt so bad that I went home that night and I cried like a baby. I was disappointed in myself because I knew what was being offered to me, and I wanted the other thing more. I repented for rejecting Christ's offer, and on March 23, 2012, I accepted the call into ministry. When I said yes, I felt such a peace about it. I knew it was what I was supposed to do. Here Christ is trying to get my life together, and I am still trying to figure it out. I put a relationship in the back of my mind and put ministry at the forefront.

Saying yes to God is not always easy to do. Growing up, you hear, have faith in God, and he will give you the desires of your heart. Anything that you want just to ask him for it, and he will make it happen. I took that to heart because now I belong to him, and I can ask what I will, and he will bring it to pass. Since moving to Georgia, I was without a car, so I needed something to drive. My mother had a car, and she would let me use it, and I felt like I needed to have my own car. The car that I had I sold it when I moved. I had faith, and I was one way to the dealership. I had been working on my job for a little while now, and I could afford a car payment. I had needs as well as the kids, and we needed a car. I get to the dealership, and I see a cream-colored Ford Edge. Anyone who knows me knows that that is the car I always said I wanted. I picked it out, and by faith, I was driving off the lot with that car. I go in with my brother, and I tell the salesman what I wanted.

I didn't need to look because I already have it in mind. He goes and does some numbers and comes back and tells me that I needed a co-signer. My mouth dropped, and I was devastated. I could not believe that he is telling me that I needed a co-signer when I have faith with me. I thanked him for his time and went home and bawled my eyes out. What had I done wrong? I did what the people told me to do, and I walked away with nothing? This can't be my life right now. God knows I need this, and this is what he does. I don't want to talk about faith to no one because obviously, it does not work like that.

I tell my mom what happened, and she says I knew you were not going to get it. Say what now? Come again? You knew I was going to walk away with nothing, and you allowed me to go down there and look like a fool? What kind of mother are you? That's what is going through my head. I didn't say those words, or I would not be here to write this book. My mom knew my faith was not where it needed to be, but she could not interfere with the lesson that God was teaching me. I can accept that as truth because I know how he gets on me if I interfere with my children and the lessons he has for them, but it does not feel good. My mom explained that I had to develop my faith more in God before it would come to pass. I wasn't happy about it, but for now, I guess I must accept it for what it is. We all have lessons that we have to go through if we want to become a better person in the long run. This was no different. Waiting on God to come through for you can be a bit challenging. I didn't want to wait. I felt like I had waited long enough. I wanted it now. If it is my blessing, release it like they said you would so I could inherit it. Some things must take place before the stuff comes. I realized that this was going to take more prayer and understanding, and I was up for the challenge.

I still had not preached my initial sermon, so I was getting prepared for that. I was so nervous because this was a big task to take on, and I didn't want to let anyone down, especially God. His word and calling are nothing to play with. Being that I come from a background of preachers, this would appear to be a walk in the park. Well, let me tell you, it wasn't. I felt the pressure of delivering the right message because of who my parents are. They are both pastors and ministers in the gospel. My dad is a preaching machine, and my mom is a teaching machine. That's quite the combination right there. Throw in my pawpaw the general in ministry and my missionary grannie, you better have some word and power to go along with you. I did not want to do the name a disservice, so the pressure was on. I studied day in and day out to get the right words for this sermon. I had invited family and friends to come down to Rome to be a witness to this event. I was contemplating what I should preach about, and literally the day before my initial sermon was to be brought forward, he gave me my title. It is time to lose some weight. I didn't know at the time that this was more than just an initial sermon. This was the title for my next season. God will give you the title to your next season before you even get there. He never leaves us in the dark. We must trust him when he shines the light on an area. I spent the next few years getting rid of the weight.

Removing yourself from your homeland doesn't mean your homeland is out of you. I may have traveled miles away from them, but my heart was till towards them. You think that going away to better yourself that people would be happy for you and eager to see the transformation in your life and celebrate it. It is not always the case, and most of the time, it is quite the opposite. Accepting Christ into your life puts you in a different category that you did not prepare for. You want to still entertain the same people without the drugs, alcohol, and promiscuity. We want people to continue to see us as the fun person we once were. We may not party like a rock star, but I am still funny.

I didn't realize that a change had come over me. Other people will see the transition while you are still looking at yourself through the same lenses. I remember going to a cookout, and I had been around these people for a long time. Here I am still trying to fit in, and I was changed to stand out. I felt ostracized again, and I didn't want to feel like that. I am still the same person, so I thought, and nobody is really interacting with me. I didn't know what to do after that. I left that place feeling like why should I even bother coming back? Nobody wants me around, so I should just go on with my life. I didn't know that this was a part of the process, and moving away was not just about leaving the city, but it was also about leaving behind the people as well. I could not bring them with me and where they are is where they needed to be. For now, I would continue to press forward, and hopefully, one day, they will come back around and accept me again.

Believe it or not, I am now making progress. I have started a new job, and I was in a better place, spiritually. Now that I have Christ in my life and on my side, I needed to explore some

things. I wanted to start doing things that would make me feel better about myself. I was making a little more money than before, and I could afford to do more. I would go to the mall after getting paid and buy the kids some things. It felt good to be able to support myself and not have to depend on others. This walking with God stuff was turning out to be ok. I am living my best life, and I love it. Nothing can get me down now.

GIVE IT AWAY

The word began to come alive in my heart, and I wanted to know more about hearing from him. People will tell you that he talks in a still small voice, or he talks in your head voice. For me, all of that seemed foreign, and I did not know anything about hearing from him. I only had word of mouth, so I was starting from scratch with this one. My mom gave me a book about hearing God's voice, and she said it would help me. I dove right in with reading it because I was about to hear him clear as day, and he was going to say my name aloud. The more I read, the more frustrated I became. Why am I not hearing him call my name? Can he not hear me and what I am asking him? I would ask him for extra money to do things for the kids, but it seemed as if I never received an answer. How was I ever going to master this if I did not know what I was listening for? I would get so frustrated and stay in bed for three days. Usually, it would start on a Friday, and I would not be myself again until Monday. It was bad, and I knew that something needed to break before I just give up totally.

I was walking through the mall, and I went and picked up something for the kids. It probably was some shirts because that's all I seemed to ever buy. You can't have enough t-shirts. I walked out of the store, and I heard, was that a need or a want? At first, I was like was that me talking to myself. Being that I wasn't thinking on those lines, I responded it was a need. God asked again, was that a need or a want? I replied, well, I wanted them to have them. He said, but was it a need? I said no, it was not. I felt like they needed them, so I went and bought them. I should be able to buy them something with the money I worked for. God told me he wanted to do that for them. I could not understand his logic because I am their mother and I am supposed to take care of them, so how would that make me look? God wanted me to realize that it is not always about providing for them yourself but allowing him to provide for us all.

I felt good because I finally heard him for myself. I wanted to hear him more, so I stayed talking to him regularly. I didn't know it was a dialogue and not a monologue. I would even write things down for him to read later. I know it sounds corny, but it worked. I got to the point where I could hear him say give it away. Now, wait a minute. You want me to do what? Give away my money? Now you are taking it to the extreme. I have kids, and they have needs. How am I going to make sure their needs are met? This is the faith God was talking about building up in me when the car situation did not work out. You must trust him even when you can't trace him. God knows exactly what it takes to get you to the level of faith you need for your purpose. I found myself paying my part of the bills and taking the rest and giving it to the church. By the time I was finished, I would have nothing but peace over my life. Never in my life had I done something like this without feeling irresponsible. I was eager to give because I was happy to hear him talking to me. It was not easy because you have kids looking at you and saying I don't have it does something to your soul. But how will you ever trust God if you never trust God? He will never let you down. I was so used to doing it all that he took away my responsibility and placed it upon his shoulders. It was a great help and a greater struggle to accept. In the days to come, I would be faced with leaning on this principal even the more.

The constant fear of the unknown will drive anyone insane. I would question what would happen to my children if I did not provide for them? How would they be able to experience the things in life that I did not get to experience? I began to put pressure on myself to produce a result that God did not put on me. While he tries to take things from my plate, here I am, piling on more stuff that I didn't have a place for. Hearing God was exciting, but it was also traumatizing, to say the least. He would ask me to do things I had no intention of doing. I wanted to hold on to those things and receive the new things he had in store for me. I could not do both. You either are going to love God or mammon. You can't serve them both. You will either love one or hate the other. It is a choice you make repeatedly. Every day I would wake up, I would choose him, but it's not to say that I didn't have an attitude.

Growing up in a home that was all about Jesus made you not want to serve him at times. Don't get me wrong I knew who he was I just didn't know exactly what he came to do. Those moments of not knowing proved to be a challenge for me later in life. I was thinking that faith was simply asking, and it would be delivered was obtaining evidence under false pretenses. There was more to it than meets the eye or what they tell you during the youth group at church. All I knew about church were you go on Sunday, Monday, Tuesday, Wednesday, Thursday, Friday, Saturday, and start it all over again. I knew about casting out demons and spirits, but I did not know how to recognize one in yourself. God was speaking to that part of me that did not line up with his way of thinking. Giving things away, especially money, was my way of getting to know him. I had to know why I was in a relationship in the first place. Was I there for what I could get only, or did I want him for who he truly was? The more I read about him, the more I wanted him. I was willing to put away anything that would separate us.

LET HIM GO

There comes the point in your life where you must let bygone be bygone. After being alone for quite some time, I started back talking to an old flame. Alex was the person who was always there for me when I needed a boost in my self-esteem. He made me feel important, and like I could do anything. I felt beautiful with him, and I knew he would always be there if I needed anything or anyone. Time had gone by, and surely, Alex appeared to be a changed man. He said he found Christ just like I had, and now we should be able to start a new life together in the right direction. Alex knew how I felt about sex and waiting, and he was on board. I felt like this could be the one. I prayed and asked God to reveal some things, and sure enough, he did just that. I was ecstatic about getting married one day, and we would have a bright future ahead of us. Everything was going great until one day, I am at work, and one of the children's grandmother walked in. I had met Rhonda before, and she was always so pleasant with me. I loved it when she came in because she would keep it real with you. On this day, I had asked God to show me if this is the person I should be with. When Rhonda came in, she started talking about her past and how God had blessed her despite her hard headedness. Of course, now my ears are wide open because she is opening up about her experience with a man she should not have been with. Rhonda told us that a woman told her not to marry that person because God was going to show her something different. If Rhonda would be patient, he had something better in store.

Being that she wanted this more than anything, Rhonda ignored the warning and proceeded with the relationship. It ended badly, and she went through some unnecessary drama because she did not wait. At that moment, I knew she was talking to me. Even though I wanted the relationship to work, I needed to step away from it so that God could show me what he had in store for me. I waited a few days to ponder on that word/warning, and then I told him. I let Alex know that I was feeling a pull away from this relationship to focus on my walk with God. Being that he said he wanted the same thing, we could let it go and work on ourselves so that we can be better for each other in the long run. That was not what he wanted, and Alex did not want anything to do with me going forth. Because I waited for God to show me something important, I was able to shift my focus on him without feeling guilty. Again, I felt the peace I needed to keep pressing forward. I ended that year released from the weight of holding on to something because it is familiar. When something is for you, you won't have to choose. It will flow with what you have going on. You don't have to change who you are to receive from someone else when God had it already planned out.

WHAT I LEARNED

Change will be visible to the outside world before you can see it in your world. You don't know what you look like and therefore you can't understand why people don't want to be around you. It is not a rejection but a sign that you are headed in the right direction. It limits the baggage you take with you into your next place in your journey. People, places, and things are not necessary for the first part of your journey. You will get rid of the responsibility that you put on yourself that God never intended for you to carry. It takes you being honest with yourself about where you want to be in your life. I know it does not always make sense, and you may not understand what he is asking of you, but it does work for your good. He that has begun a work in you is faithful to complete it. We should be open to the voice so that he can guide us according to what he sees and not what we see. For God knows the plans he has for you, and sometimes those plans do not include everybody, you know.

God will give you the strength to walk away, even when staying is easier. If you want what God has for you, you must make those tough decisions to keep following until you receive it. Don't allow the familiar to be the only thing you ever know. There is so much more out there to explore.

Chapter Three
GO

By this time in my life, I don't know what to expect, but I know that God requires something more significant than I was ready to give. I just don't know what to do, so I just keep reading, praying, and fasting. The more I read, the more I am feeling the sense to go. I have no idea where to go, but I must leave where I am now. It doesn't mean I had to leave the state, but something in me would not allow me to rest.

Often God would speak a one-word sentence to me, and I was trying my best to figure out what it all meant. I started going to different places I thought he wanted me to go to. I was clueless, and I did not want to make a mistake or hear wrong, so I just sat on that word. I continued with my journey as if he never spoke a word. The only problem is that it would get louder and louder. I could not shut it off, and he would not allow me to forget it. God has a way of getting you to the place he wants you to be. He will use people, the radio, a child, or even a billboard to speak to you, especially if you are running from what he is saying. I sat on this word for about a year because I was so afraid of being wrong. Nothing says embarrassment like speaking on something, and then it does not produce like you said. I wanted to avoid that. I had done enough of speaking and not producing, and this time I was attaching God's name to it. I had to be careful and prayerful because of how time-sensitive this word was.

Going is not always easy because you can't just up and leave your responsibilities on others. God gave them to us, and we don't get to just neglect them because we have a word for the Lord. These were the thoughts that were going through my head. I was not sure of what to think about making this type of faith step. I had done nothing of this magnitude before, and now I am being pressured to give him a yes. Well, not so much pressured but assured that it will be ok to follow this leading. I must have had a moment of clarity because once I said yes, there was no turning back.

Just like I had left the other job within a week, I found myself faced with this circumstance again, only to be walking away from employment. Now, I know you are wondering how in the world was she supposed to do this when clearly, she is the mother of four children who depend on her for everything? Listen, I was thinking those same things myself, and it was no walk in the park. I tell you. You don't know what is going to happen. You are walking into the unknown without any further instructions. You have one word, and it does not produce anything tangible yet. How are the kids going to eat? Who will clothe them? How are the bills going to get paid now that you are on this tangent about following God? I don't know how he is going to do it, but I am crazy enough to trust him.

Making up your mind is the hardest thing you will ever do because you are trying to figure out the outcome before you get started. Until your heart and mind align with each other, your feet will not move. I noticed this every time I wanted to say yes, the heartstrings would be pulled, and I would back out again. What kind of a mother would I be if I let them down? I did not want to disappoint them and come up short again. This would tear me apart, and I would go back in hiding for a month or so and then revisit the word. It wasn't until I had bible study with the kids and my nephew Tyler, and we were reading from Mark 2 when the disciples were being called. They left everything to follow Christ because they were called from their jobs to follow him. It wasn't until he said it is an honor to be called by God that I understood the word go. That did it for me. It was a Saturday morning, and then on the following Monday, I put in my one week notice on my job. I told my boss that I was going into ministry full time and this would be my last week. She looked at me and said I will not stand in God's way if that's what he is asking of you. I felt such peace after those words, and I could not believe how easy it was once I surrendered to the call to come higher and go. I don't know what this looks like and where I would end up, but I was more than ready to find out. Nothing was going to stop me from finding out what he had in store.

WHERE AM I?

You would think that after he tells you something like go that he would have this detailed plan laid out for you to follow. Absolutely not. I had nothing, and after I went, I was in a place I did not know with nothing but the word to guide me. After leaving my job, I was invited to preach at a service in my hometown, and I was excited about going. I was preparing and looking forward to the experience. It would be my first time preaching in my hometown that I could remember. I received my paycheck, and after paying the bills, I realized that I did not have any extra money to make it up the road. I didn't want to ask anyone for the money because I'm supposed to be following God, and it is now his responsibility to take care of me. Immediately I began to panic and question my move. I messed up and now look at me, looking like a fool for following God. Later that day, I received a call from Linda saying that they needed help getting their children to school for the week. She said she would pay me and being that I needed some money quickly, I agreed. After leaving my job, I ended up being a caretaker of a child who still attended there. Going back, there was weird because I left the job, and now, I'm again picking up a child. I was embarrassed at first, but I quickly remembered what I had to do later in the week. I swallowed my pride and kept showing up until Linda didn't need me anymore. When it came time for her to pay me, something went wrong at the bank, and it would be the following week before she could pay me. I felt so bad that I did not even know how to respond. I didn't want to seem desperate for the money, but I was desperate for the money. Doubt came in like a flood, and I just started to bawl my eyes out. I could not believe this was happening to me. I took a step of faith only to get knocked back to where I started. I cried out to God, and I said you told me to go and I did. I don't need to look like a fool. Please come through for me. It's too late for me to turn back now. I was supposed to leave on that Friday morning in time to get there for the Friday night service. Early that morning, I received the phone call that I could come and pick up the money Linda owed me. I could not get there fast enough. I was so thankful to God that he supplied my need. I didn't have to ask anyone for the money, and I went and did what thus said the Lord.

People don't understand how hard it is to stand on God's word with no evidence. It is like you are holding a conversation with yourself, and people walk by you as if you are crazy. Faith is something we preach about, but we rarely see it walked out in this magnitude. I had something to fall back on when walking by faith. My mom moved to a new city on faith in what God told her. He opened doors for her, so I was just following in her footsteps. I wanted to do what she did to experience God like I never had. I had no idea how lonely it is on this journey. Even those who you think would be there for you, turn their back on you because you have now left logic and gone into a place that God does not travel in very often. These are the things people would say to me. I heard God wrong, and I needed to go back again. God doesn't move like that, especially when you have children, or he would provide you with more so that you can accomplish what he is asking of you. I could not believe the people of faith who had so much doubt in God's ability to take care of us. It almost cost me my mind. Mental torment is real, and if you are not careful, it will take you off your course and eventually out of this world. Believing in something or someone you have never seen is crazy talk, but look at how many people in the bible followed God without a backup plan?

How many people left behind what they knew to go to a place of unfamiliar? Abraham is the father of all nations. He left his homeland, his family, and everything he knew to follow a God he only heard about. The disciples left all they had known to follow someone they heard about. Elisha followed Elijah after he tossed a mantle upon him. So many examples are in place through the word of God that shows us that a word is all you need to follow God. You must know about him and who he is to even think about going beyond the norm. That is why reading the word so much in my first two years of following him was important because I needed to know who this man was. I had to know that if I would just put my trust in him and give him a chance, I would come out better than when I started. I didn't have a choice because I told him I would go even if I had to go by myself. I took my vow to him very seriously, and if I was going to see the promises of God, I had to move in purpose.

Nobody could tell me exactly what to expect because everyone's journey is different. They could not speak for me, and neither could they deny me access to my inheritance. They had no right to interfere with what God was doing in my life, and I, for one, was not about to let that happen. I have always been stubborn, but this time I was steadfast, unmovable, always abounding in the word of the Lord knowing that my labor was not in vain. I was tired of starting and stopping, and I was going to finish something. Either way, I wasn't coming off the path until he told me to. I wasn't going to let anything separate me from the love of God. He had been too good to me so far. I was in it for better or for worse, and oh how it got worse before it got better.

We can be so sure of ourselves that we forget that there is a price to pay even for all that knowledge. I was so sure that God called me for something better, and I knew it would not be long before he would ask something of me in more dept. I don't know when I became so sure of myself, but it happened, and I ran with it.

HEALING BEGINS

God truly has a way of getting my attention through everyday situations, and this time it was no different. It is now January 2015, and I am feeling the need to connect to other people outside of my current circle. One of my Facebook friends, Charlotte, began to post statuses from a gentleman who was in tune with the mind of a man. She would post them, and I would begin to like and follow this gentleman. I liked his style, and Dameon had a heart for single people. Single people get looked down upon sometimes because we are single, but no one wants to really help us out of our dark places. We must depend on the Lord for help, so Dameon's words of wisdom were refreshing. I could sense God pushing me to meet new people outside of my current circle. Even though it was just Facebook, it had a purpose in my life.

One day Dameon mentioned that he, along with two other

people, were starting a group by the name of SANA. It stands for single and not ashamed. At that moment, I knew this was for me. I did not want to pass up this opportunity. At this time, I was home all day reading and praying, and I needed to interact with some people outside of my family. I stepped out of my comfort zone and told him to add me. Again, I had no idea what to expect, but I was expecting to at least learn how to cope with being single. Being around other like-minded people was what I needed because some people just don't understand.

I joined, and I was eager to see what the group had to offer me. I wasn't sure if I was going to post or comment, but I would be there to glean from others who were not too shy to post. One day I would get up the nerve to say something, but for now, I am just a spectator. To my surprise, there were more people there who were stepping out of their comfort zone than I thought. It was refreshing to hear others go beyond the borders of their comfort zone and see what the world has to offer. There were people from across the United States and eventually from around the world. I met people from London, Australia, the Bahamas, and even Africa. It became a fast-growing place for singles who were not ready to mingle but to get the message of Jesus Christ out there in a way that would encourage them to keep going. I could not believe it. Before I knew it, I was posting in the group, commenting and getting to know people from all walks of life. I tell you God indeed showed himself mighty through this group because everything about it was divine. It was a prayer answered that I did not discuss with anyone. I met some amazing women who I am still friends with up until now. Only God could orchestrate something of this magnitude.

The group became an instant hit, and other things begin to come from it. Women ministries and men ministries were formed, and love and relationship groups were popping up. Whatever you needed, you could find it in SANA. It wasn't a hookup site for people to find their soulmate, but people developed relationships outside of the group and eventually married. It was mind-blowing and needed at that time. People were experiencing healing and began to understand their purpose and calling on their lives. The deliverance would take place right on a person's post, and we would go on for hours about the goodness of the Lord. I was learning so much, and God was right there during it all, making sure I was not walking away the same way I came. I could not believe what was accomplished in months that would have taken me years to do if I had done it myself. God was showing up and showing out daily. I was so hungry for God. I could not get enough of what he was doing in the group. Eventually, the calling would come forth, and I would branch out into something I had never done before.

CALI'S CALLING

God was showing me who I was, and I was becoming comfortable with him and hearing him when he instructs me to do something. After all the healing was taking place, the women still needed something more. I was pumped and excited about seeing the women made free, and I could not wait until there was a place we could share our stories and testimonies of healing, deliverance, and overcoming the cares of this world. I got with one other lady, Shameka, who was feeling the same way I was. She could not contain the joy she had experienced and wanted the women to experience a deeper level of healing. How would we do this, seeing that this is something we have not done before? All I know is we said yes, and the rest is history. We formed the group Touch the Hem, which was to reach the cry in the crowd. We had weekly teachings and prayer calls that would usher in the spirit of the living God. So many people would join us and receive the confirmation, the courage, the strength to continue their journey, and not give in to what is surrounding them. For some, it was the first time that they were able to see themselves just like God sees them. It was a beautiful thing to behold. There were days I would sit in awe of who God is by how he was using us to help others. All I wanted was to be used by him to bring others to freedom. I had no idea that it would go as far as it did to the point, we ended up doing a conference in California.

I had never been to this place, but I wasn't about to miss out on it.

We decided to do a three-day conference in the summer of 2016 that would feature the leadership team. I had no idea how I was going to make it there, but I knew I was going. I began to call those things that were not as though they were. People would ask me in the months leading up to it was I still going. They knew I did not have a job, but I kept the faith and kept right on speaking it from the heart. Deep down inside, I had no clue who was going to give me the money or how I was going to raise it. Working for it didn't seem like the way, so I just kept trusting God and seeking His face. Those were the instructions he had for me. Seek ye first the kingdom of God and his righteousness, and all these things would be added unto you. I was looking for him to add while I worked on seeking him. I must admit. It did look crazy for a minute. People said you can't even take care of your own kids, but you out here going to California. I didn't lose my faith though it hurt my feelings. When are we going to start trusting him instead of questioning everything he says? At some point, you must block out the naysayers and move in closer to what he is saying.

It is now early May 2016, and the conference is in late June 2016. I am still in my faith, believing God for the finances to get to California. I do not want to look stupid in front of these people because I am following you. I remember one of the ladies from our group who worked for an airline. I needed to find out how much I needed for airfare. I had to have some numbers to present to God or whoever he was going to use to get me to California. I reached out to Kimberly and asked her how much a round-trip ticket would be from North Carolina to California. She messaged me back and said it would be $800. I was like, wow. That's a lot of money, and I am nowhere near having any of that. I thanked her and went on about my business. Shortly after that, Kimberly messaged me and said if you don't mind flying stand by, I can send you a ticket, but you would need to fly out of Atlanta. I immediately said yes and then asked, what is standing by?

Stand by is where you have a ticket, but you don't have a seat. You are guaranteed to get on a flight if there are seats available. You still must choose a flight, but if that flight is full, you will get bumped back to the next one. That would keep happening until you finally get a seat. Stand by. I agreed to it, and she directed me to the flights that were leaving out on the day I chose. I spoke it into the atmosphere that every flight I chose, I would be on. I realized that this, too, was a part of the faith walk, and I had to be firm in what I believed.

My brother Jay and his wife Nancy, drove me to the airport early that Monday morning. I was nervous because I had heard the horror stories about the TSA lines and how I needed to be there hours before my flight left. I arrived at 5 and was in line for 5 minutes. I had plenty of time to kill. One of the things God spoke to me while waiting was I had to act as if I already had a seat on the plane. I could not be nervous but confident in my choosing. I would pack up when I saw the others pack up and be ready to board just like everyone else. I checked like everyone else, and I waited. When I heard the flight being called over the intercom, I gathered my things and got in position. The enemy tried to distract me with his lies, but I was too focused on the promise to be burdened with his problems. I held my belongings close, and when they called my name, I boarded the plane like a boss. I sat with a lady who was from Rome, and we talked and had a wonderful time on the ride to California.

I had never been on a plane before this, and I was riding like a pro. Here I am going to a place unknown to me but known to my father, who orchestrated this whole thing from the beginning to the end. I had a full ride to a place that I had dreamed of. Only God could do this. I touched down and met one of my Sana sisters, Shenea, for the first time. It was as if I had known her all my life, and she treated me like family. Not one time did I have to worry about what I was going to eat, how I was going to get to the hotel, and I was even able to go to the beach and behold the beauty of the Lord. I am still in awe until this day for how God continued to show himself in my life because I heard the word and went.

WHAT I LEARNED

The unknown is your friend because your God is going before you to make sure that nothing happens to you that will not help you. His word said that he has nothing but good for you and not for evil. He has an expected end that is beneficial for you in the long run. If you never take a step of faith, how will you ever see the glory of God? Staying in the box will only limit you and not God. If I had not followed the word go, I would still be stuck on the what if. At some point, you just must put all your eggs in his basket, close your eyes, take his hand, and walk it out. In Joshua, he said to be of good courage. As I was with Moses, so shall I be with thee. You cannot go wrong when you have a word from the Lord. One word can change your life if you allow it. Even if that word is Go.

We like to believe that God will not allow anything to happen to us because we have children. If that were the case, many children would not be without their parents today. God's plan may not look like yours, but his plan is fail-proof. You must come into agreement with him and give him full control. It may hurt, but don't lose your faith.

Chapter Four
HEALING IN THE GO

When I returned home from my trip, my eyes had been opened to amazing things. I realized I had just flown across the country for free. I did not pay for anything other than one dinner with the ladies, and I came home with a balance on my card. I saw God in a way I had never seen him before. He was, indeed, my provider. He carried me across the water into a territory that I was not familiar with. He gave me favor in the land, and when I left, my hands were clean, and I was free to press forward. I did not know what the future would hold, but if it was anything like what I had just experienced, I was not getting off the ride until I had received it all.

Just like the ten lepers who were healed as they walked away, I was being encouraged to keep walking to receive more healing in the areas I was praying about. By this time, I did not know that I needed any more healing, but God knows and sees all. He gets in the places that no one can see and uproots the things that were buried under other stuff. I had to take off the layers and get to the root of things that was keeping me bound. Because of the way my faith was set up, I needed this for real.

Being that I was so used to being by myself, I did not know when someone was taking notice of me. It was as if I was hidden, and nobody could see me. It did not matter how good I looked on the outside, no one was taking notice of me. I began to think that something was wrong with me, and I needed to change something about my outside. Unbeknownst to me, it was my inner man that needed a make-over. I could not tell exactly what I needed, but something had to be done.

Joining the single and not ashamed group allowed me to get to know so many people quickly. There were plenty of guys in the group, and I often wondered if one of them was my husband. I would not post anything about me personally or that I was even seeking companionship. I knew my husband would know who I was and that he would have to come correct. I did not have time for games or drama, and if you were not about that married life, I am not the one for you. As I am going on about my day, I get an inbox from a gentleman by the name of Austin, and he says hello. At first, I was hesitant to respond because I was not sure of how to take his interaction. Eventually, I responded with a hello, and Austin proceeds to tell me he noticed me. I was like, what did you say. I never had those words spoken to me in that way, so I was open to receive more from him. Austin tells me that he saw me in the group, and he liked how I was all about the Lord. He admired my knowledge of the word and how much faith I had in God. I was wondering if he was talking about the same person he was chatting with. I was just myself, but I did not know anyone was taking notice. I thanked him for his kind words and continued my journey. Austin would reach out from time to time on my post or in my inbox to check on me or to ask why he had not seen any of my posts in the group. I felt like he was stalking me a little, but I did not allow that to deter me. All I knew, he could be the one for me.

I recently had received a word for birthing new things, and shortly after this, Austin entered the picture. I wanted to be open to God as much as possible because he can do anything but fail. If he can part the red sea, surely, he can send me the husband he has for me, so I was not taking any chances on missing out. We exchanged numbers, and we began to talk daily. Austin was very affluent in the word and his knowledge of the scriptures. He pastored for some years and had come off an assignment and just waiting on the Lord. He didn't have any children; that was a big plus for me. Austin seemed to be in tune with the Lord and wanted what he wanted. I started to see myself with him and us becoming a family. I was even talking about moving where he was at if things moved into that direction. For me, I was sold on this man of God. All I needed was for him to ask me, and I was ready. Even though I had not known him very long, I was prepared to jump on board and make it official. That's when things started going south.

I noticed that whenever I would make a post about something that did not pertain to him, Austin would immediately become upset and disconnect from me. This would confuse me and cause me to look at myself. I did not believe I said anything wrong, so I wanted to fix it almost immediately. He would not take responsibility for his actions, but I would stay and try to figure it all out. This would frustrate me to the point I did not want to deal with him anymore. What was so wrong with me that I could not keep a man hundreds of miles away happy? This is precisely where God wanted me to be. God showed me that some areas were still tied with my past and the root of rejection. I would shut down, trying to make myself more presentable for that person. Nothing I did was good enough, and this person made those old feelings resurface. It was a good thing and a bad thing because who wants to face themselves in a way that others are not doing it. How come he gets to get off scot-free, and here I am struggling to stay afloat, and I must apologize. I did not know at the time Goad was preparing me for my husband, and someone must help you get there. You won't get there by yourself. Those counterfeits have a purpose. Just like Judas, Jesus needed him because his betrayal leads to our recovery. If he had not participated in the betrayal, we would not have been a part of the redemption. All things work together for good, but it does not feel good when you are going through.

Another thing I had to learn to deal with was silence. Austin was very good at giving me the silent treatment. When I began to look at the root of the silence, it showed me that again, silence meant rejection. I knew when someone was not coming back because they would be here today, gone tomorrow. No warning, no signals. They would vanish into thin air, and I would not see them or hear from them again. You know what that does to a person's self-esteem? It can have devastating effects on how we interact with others, especially those of the opposite sex. I would do all I could to prevent them from leaving, but nothing would work. Silence was my enemy, and I felt that I did not want to interact with it at all. If no one were ever silent again, I would be fine. Lord, how am I going to get through the silence? One day at a time and one thought at a time.

I had to learn to see my worth in me. Silence is not the problem; their understanding is. They could not see the need for me, so, therefore, it was nothing to cut me off. Anything that you believe, that does not add any value to your life, you leave behind. If a person is not mature enough to tell you this, they will just leave you and hope that you won't notice that they are no longer there. It's as if you did something wrong, but they don't have the guts to let you know what it is. Many times, I did nothing wrong, but because he did not need me, the want was not enough. You can want something, but it's not until it becomes a need that you pursue it until it is in your possession. He sought after what he wanted but had no idea, I was really what he needed.

God had to redirect me in a way that I became more secure in myself. I did not go out and buy new shoes, clothes, jewelry, or even give myself a make-over. I went deeper in prayer and deliverance so that I would be able to live after the disappointment. I wanted us to work because I saw what he could not see. I loved him even before he knew it. I just could not make him receive what the spirit was showing him. He needed a friend, but he wanted a wife. I wanted a husband, but I needed healing. One without the other will bring you back to that same place until you surrender to the latter one. The internal revenue goes inside your finances to see where you are financially and how much you will owe or receive from them. Depending on where you are, you could end up owing them thousands of dollars because of the tax bracket you are in. It's the same way in the spirit. You must know where you are because sometimes it may end up costing you more than you wanted to invest, and if you are not careful, your circumstances could end up leaving you broken and owing them in the end. I could not afford another round of this, so I had to do what was necessary to get me to the place that God was leading me to.

Austin kept disappearing and reappearing, and the whole time God was walking out my healing one incident at a time. I was no longer afraid of being rejected because I knew rejection was for my protection. The more Austin pulled away, the further I got. All he was doing was opening the path to my freedom. Years of being stuck and on the marry-go-round of in out of situation ships were coming to an end, and I had Austin to thank. I had to have a father forgive him moment because he knows not what he does. The freedom that came through this journey allowed me to love myself even more and to appreciate the flaws that so many had rejected. I could not believe the doors that would open from me, just simply showing love to those who despitefully use you.

Time is passing me by, and I must enter a season of rest. I could no longer fight for my life but to lay it down. I did not understand the instructions, but again here I am obeying without a blueprint. I knew I had to move because the pressure was becoming too much to produce a result that I was not ready for. People would try to pressure me into doing things that were not ordained by God. Many times, I was called lazy, crazy, unfit mom, and the devil, to say the least. I could not continue like this because, at some point, I would explode. I used to get up early in the mornings and go for a bike ride. It was a part of what God had me doing as a way of disciplining me. I would go to the local track and walk until he says stop and then come back home. One morning I was talking with him, and I did not want to interrupt the things he had going forth in the lives of those around me. I told him to help because doing his will was the only thing that mattered to me. He told me that when your father tells you to leave, then it is time to go. I received those words in my spirit and went home to start my day. A month later, I was searching for a place to live because school was getting ready to begin again, and I would need a place for us to stay. As I am preparing for the new year, my father comes to me and says it is time for you to leave. Immediately I knew God had spoken through him to tell me that another change was coming. It was not the outcome I wanted, but it is God's plan and his timing. I agreed, and I packed up a backpack and left and went to a friend's house.

That day I had no idea where I was going because I did not want to go back where I came from, but what else could I do. The doors were closing, and nothing else was opening full time. I could not stay in this place because I was needed somewhere else. I kept fighting to stay above water when all I must do was give in to the lifeguard and his instructions. I was not going to drown, and I just needed to reach out and grab a hold to the lifeline. It hurt my heart to have to be rescued, but I needed to live to fight another day.

HEALING IN THE GOING BACK

After returning to Georgia, I was bitter, upset, and embarrassed because I had to return to the one place that I believed that God took me from. How could he do me like this, and I had nothing to show for it? I was supposed to be farther along and at least have some proof that God is speaking to me and not just out here winging it for the sake of doing something. I could not go back to just sitting at the house because things were different now, and everybody is looking at you to see what you must bring to the table. I did not want to talk, and I did not want to explain myself because you would not understand, anyway. My mother tried to talk to me, but I did not want any sound advice right now because I just want to be in my feelings. Why don't I have anything to show God? How come I am still out here looking crazy? At some point, you are going to have to come through for me. I can't go on like this.

As I am sitting in the living room, my son Taye tells me that he ran into my old boss. She asked if we were back and if I needed a job that I should come to see her. Now mind you, I have not seen this lady in two years, and I did not ask for the job. I was sitting there complaining, and my 18-year-old son says, Mom, did you ask for the door? I said no. He said, did you even go after the door? I said no. He said, well, just walk through it. You never know what may happen. I could not say anything, but you're right. I don't know why I'm back, but here I am, and someone is asking me to come back there without even filling out an application. I follow his instructions, and I go see her. I still have an attitude because I really don't want to be here, but here I am. She says she could use me, but I only wanted to substitute. I wasn't ready to commit just yet. I needed to keep my schedule open just in case God had this fantastic assignment for me to complete, and I did not need to be tied down doing anything other than that. I was not about to miss my blessing for no one. That attitude I had was about to get me out of all the blessings he had in store. I had to swallow my pride and get myself together and quickly.

As I began to sub, I begin to let go of the anger. I started seeing God for who he is, and he knows exactly where I am. He knows what I need to receive all that he had in store for me. I could not continue to act as if I knew more than he does, and I could do a better job at fulfilling the things on my checklist. I had to humble myself under his hand because, at any moment, he could change my entire life around. I could only see what is in front of me, but he can see the ending. Swallowing my pride was hard, but I did it. I took a step back and stepped up in the place he had prepared for me. I became content with the situation I was in. I no longer needed to lead. I became a faithful follower of him. If I did not know how to play follow-the-leader before, I found out how to play after this. I started having joy with the little things. I knew my returning was not the same as my beginning there. It was all God both times, but this time I was on an assignment and not just there to get a paycheck. There would be some great things that would come out of me staying the course that God prepared for me. I had to be patient and allow him to bring it to pass.

WHAT I LEARNED

The obedience in a thing is better than the sacrifice of a thing. God requires obedience from those who say that he is our God. Instructions are given for us to carry out. It is not time for us to negotiate the terms for which you are to fulfill them. Each time we kick against the prick, we are delaying ourselves from discovering the truth about ourselves. Every time we decide to run and not face the things that scare us, we will continue in a cycle that will have us going in circles and never breaking the curse. A marry-go-round life should not continue once you find out the truth. You should want to hop off the wheel that others keep spinning. No one should have that much power over you, and you are not benefitting from them. You must be willing to learn the lesson and graduate at some point.

Opportunities are already in place for you. You must get to that place so that you can see that God was telling the truth the whole time. God isn't trying to empress the people who don't believe. He is trying to build the ones who do. Many people don't understand the journey because they did not stick with it long enough to get the plans God had in store for them. So, they will try to deter you from getting to that place called there, but you must press in to win. Following the voice of the Lord gets rid of the stress that you may feel when you are approached by people who just can't get with the program.

Healing is your portion. We were granted it on the cross, and it is up to us to receive it. You can't limit God and his ability to bring you to that place of wholeness. He has many ways to get you to that place. You must be willing to follow his lead and go where he says go. You will not get what you need by trying to organize it yourself. You need help, and depending on how deep your hurt is, it will come from the place you least expect it. Nobody wants to hurt other people, but let's face it. Hurt people hurt people just like healed people heal people. We put out what is inside of us, and if we can't see the hurt, someone will feel it down the line. God goes through us with a fine-tooth comb, and he leaves nothing behind that would hinder us. Don't be afraid of what you will find underneath all of that. God isn't going to be caught off guard. He knew it was there before the foundations of the world would be were laid. Don't try to hide it because he has a way of making things come to the surface. Just give in, and it will make your life a lot easier.

Chapter Five
LEAVING IT ALL BEHIND

At some point in your life, you must plan about what stays and what goes. Everything cannot coincide with the other, and you must draw the line somewhere in the sand. Being indecisive about your future will leave room for others to keep telling you what you will or will not do. God did not create us to be controlled by man. He was to be guided by him through his love for us. He had given us all things to enjoy, and that would help us live a peaceful life. Why should we continue to live in bondage when we were created to live free?

People will have you doing things because that is all you qualify for in their book. They can not see you beyond their limited vision, so when they speak to you, they speak from their limitations, not God. They will place you at the scene of a crime and leave you there knowing you have an alibi with them. You must take control of your destiny even if it disappoints people along the way.

I went home to visit some family members during a difficult time. I contacted Ricky, an old friend, because he told me that if I was ever in town to hit him up and we could hang out. I did that, and he said he would come and visit me. I was scheduled to leave later that evening, so I could be home by a certain time. Of course, Ricky was late, and he showed up as if he was the man of the hour. I could not believe that he would do this yet again, and I wasn't sure how much more I could take. I ended up giving him the benefit of the doubt because I did tell him about the visit last minute, so I did not say anything out the way.

As I sat there and waited, time was moving, and I had a four-hour drive ahead of me. I did not want to arrive home late and must be up early for work the next day. Ricky comes in and has this attitude about himself. As if he was doing me a favor by even showing up. He felt as if he was the man, and he should be waited for and upon. We talked briefly, and I tell him I must hit the road. He tells me to call him once I make it home, and I promised I would. We hug, and I leave his presence. The entire ride home, I thought about all the times he showed up late or not at all. How he never really made it about me and was never honest with anyone about our relationship. Ricky kept me in the dark and did not want anyone to know except for a handful of my friends. He was continually doing the disappearing act on me and giving me the silent treatment. Months and even a couple years would go by before I would hear from him. I decided that night that I would not put myself through that anymore because I simply did not have to. I got home, and I made the phone call. I told him that I arrived safely, but we needed to talk. I knew he was a good person, but this relationship could no longer exist. I needed more, and he was not ready to give that to me, and I was ok with it. I can't make you grow up, but I can remove myself from your to-do list because you have too much going on right now.

I am ready to put me first and second is not an option. If you can't give me your all, I don't want none of you. I thanked him for what we shared, but this would be the last time we go around this mountain. He understood, and we departed ways. I felt so free at that moment, even though my flesh wanted me to think that I was making a big mistake. If that were the case, he would catch up with the words that it would take for me to know that he had an encounter with him. My life would no longer be on hold for others. I am going for mine and if you don't like it, not my problem.

WHAT I LEARNED

Walking away can be hard because it is something that you must take charge of. Nobody tells you how to feel because they were left. I was used to people leaving that I never had to really face them. This time I had to walk away with the faith that God would bring the person in my life that would be able to handle showing up every time and not just when it was suitable for them. It felt amazing to be able to set the boundary and stick with it without feeling guilty. Boundaries are necessary when you are going to go forth and pursue your dreams and goals. Many people don't like the boundaries you set because now they don't have access to you like they once had. It shows that they don't really respect you if they keep crossing them. Therefore, you must make them clear and don't allow anyone leeway when it comes to your life. People will talk to you any kind of way and will expect you to adhere to them. It is not always something negative, but giving you the run around is another way for people to disrespect your boundaries. I never really had them; that is why so many people were able to come and go without a second thought. But this was the stopping point, and to gain access to my heart or anything close to me, you must fit the criteria.

So here I am again walking alone but joyful. I had released myself from a cycle that plagued my life for years. When you take back the power, and you put your faith in God, he can now trust you with the promises he spoke to you in private. There comes the point where your sacrifice must pay off. No more delay, but everything you had prayed for was on its way to your door. All you must do now is open it and receive it for once in my life. I always kept the scripture seek ye first the kingdom of God and his righteousness before me. If I were seeking him, what I was promised would find me no matter where I was because God knew exactly how to get it to me. The work I had to do was on myself first, and then he could release the things he had in store for me. Nobody will understand your private press until they see your public promise come to pass. I had fought a good fight and left everything in the hands of the Lord. I had come through the fire and the rain, and now the storm was passing over. Everything I cried for was about to show up in a way I would never have expected. This is the miracle God spoke about before my journey began. If I would just die to myself, my will, and my plans, his plans would become effective, and he would carry them out all the way. I now know that even in leaving things behind, you find yourself in front of the things you lost, but in a greater magnitude. I could not even imagine my life going in this direction, but he knew, and for that, I am grateful.

Chapter Six
THE FINALE

There are not enough words to describe the journey to finding myself. There were highs and lows along the way, and often those lows would get the best of me. I never stopped fighting, pressing, and praying for better days. Those storms were brutal, but they built me for my greater works. Standing in the place that would give me everything I needed was the ultimate pay off, and I am glad I did not lose heart before I finished.

It was April 21, 2017, and I was sitting in my room going through my phone. I wasn't looking at anything, but I had it in my hand. Shortly after that, I received a text message from one of my sisters in the Lord, Gladies. She said she was being led to introduce me to her brother. At first, I was shocked because I had known her for about two years, and we met in the group Sana. We never discussed her brothers, but we did pray for them each week. I didn't know what to say but ok. Being that I know her relationship with God, I took it seriously. She was not a woman who played with God, and her discernment was on point. I agreed to talk to him, and I went on my way.

I told God I was not in the mood to help another man find himself, encourage him, tell him how much you loved him, and build him up in the faith. I was tired, and I did not want the hassle. The last one took a lot out of me, but I gained so much from the experience that I said, not my will, but thy will be done. I did not want to disappoint God, and if he needed me to be a sister to another one of his sons, so be it. I could miss out because I am tired and not looking at the bigger picture. I didn't think I was ready for a relationship, so I was going in with a clear mind and a clear heart to help.

It took 9 days before I was able to talk to him. I began to think that he was not interested or that it must not be meant for us. All these thoughts started flooding my mind because I was used to the silence, but God would not allow me to stay there. I had dealt with it, and God had delivered me from that. I needed to be patient and wait on him to open the door of opportunity. During this time, Gladies was visiting her brother and mother. I reached out to her because I was coming to visit in a few weeks to drop off my children for the summer with their families. She told me to give her a call, and I did just that. It was April 30, 2017, and I spoke to Maurice for the first time.

We both were nervous because we did not prepare to talk, but his mother just gave him the phone, and we started talking. Maurice seemed a little shy, and I could tell it in his voice. I told him there was nothing to be nervous about. We are just brother and sister in the Lord having a conversation. There was no pressure to produce anything but to be yourself. I later found out those words allowed him to calm down and engage with a conversation with me. We did not talk any more than five minutes, and we ended the conversation. I felt like it went well, and I hoped Maurice was comfortable enough to meet up one day soon. I was becoming anxious, but again I had to wait for the time to present itself.

Gladies and I had never met in person, so I thought this would be a great way to see each other since I was going to be close to where they lived. She told me she had to get back to her home and that she would not be available. Gladies said that her mom and brother would be there and would love for me to stop by. This took me by surprise because I needed some back up for this meeting. I was comfortable meeting them if she was there, but going in by myself was asking a bit much from me. I could not continue to be nervous, so I checked with their mom and asked was the 20th of May a good day for them. They accepted my offer, and we were set to meet for the first time. I thought, Lord, what am I getting myself into? After all, I had been through, is this a good idea to meet someone who you barely know? I could not allow fear to stop me and what could go wrong. It is just a meeting. Nobody is getting married on that day. Remember you are just meeting your brother in the Lord for the first time. It is no big deal.

The first 19 days of May were filled with prayer, fasting, and seeking God for direction. I did not want to go into this without his approval or his spirit. I wanted to present myself in a way that would be pleasing in his sight. Whatever he wanted to do through this meeting was cool with me, and I am not going to stand in the way of us meeting. It does not take God a long time to execute a plan. The preparation takes longer than the execution. Once the appointed time has arrived, there is nothing else to do but show up and receive. I had a hard time receiving being that I am a giver, but I had to be reminded everything that God gives us is good and to be received with thanksgiving. I was thankful that I can meet people from all walks of life. You never know where you will end up until you allow God to take you there.

On the morning of May 19th, I packed my bags for a three-day trip. I was so nervous. I did not inform my children of my plans because I did not want to involve them in something that may not be anything. I kept it to myself until I knew it would become something more. I wanted to protect their feelings if it did not work out, and there wasn't any need to bring them into it too soon. They were just excited to be going home to visit their family and friends. The drive up there was peaceful, and I talked to God the entire time. He assured me that everything was alright and that I was in good hands. Just be me, and that was enough.

The next day I wasn't scheduled to meet them until later, so I went to a service in Greenville, South Carolina. I promised my mom I would come down for the convention at least one day, and this gave me time to prepare. I intended to go here and stay a couple of hours and head back up 85 North to Fort Mill. I had a great time at the service, and then I was invited to attend the luncheon. I kept looking at my watch, and I didn't want to be late, but I needed to grab something to eat, so I obliged. The more I tried to break away, the longer people would talk with me and keep me in that place. I knew it was a distraction, and I had to get out of there. I ended up dropping food on my clothes, and this was my opportunity to leave the luncheon. I only had clothes to travel in, and this was the outfit I was to meet Maurice and his mom in. What am I supposed to do now?

I stopped at the nearest restaurant and changed my clothes. I had my driving clothes and my clothes for service on Sunday. I opted for driving clothes. I wasn't trying to impress him with my outer. It was the inner God wanted him to see. If that wasn't good enough, Maurice wasn't the one for me. I sucked it up and got on the highway back to Gastonia. I pull over to take a break and to enter the address in the GPS. I called to make sure they were there, and I was on my way. In the back of my mind, I thought, "God don't fail me now."

THE OFFICIAL MEETING

You never know what to expect when you meet people for the first time. I saw a picture of Maurice, and he was easy on the eyes, so I wasn't concerned about that. It was more about, what would we talk about, being we only had a five-minute conversation. I didn't want it to be fake, but that the spirit would guide the conversation. I pull up, and I see this guy outside. I could not tell if it was him or not, so I called. Maurice answered and said that was him outside. I park, and he walks over to the car. I had to put on my shoes, and he walks me into the house. Instantly, we connected. We talked as if we had known each other all our lives. We were engaged in conversation. There was not a dull moment in the room. We laughed, and his mom even prayed during the meeting. The room was filled with joy and love. I had never experienced that with anyone, especially their mom. She accepted me from day one. She loved the Lord, and you could see it and feel it. His great-niece was there, and when I was getting ready to leave, I was able to pick her up. His mom said she was very picky and did not take well to strangers. Was this a sign of what was to come? Who knows? It was another moment of laughter and joy we shared before I left.

Maurice walks me to the car, and we chat for a few more minutes. We never touch, and he bids me goodnight. Peace is the only word that I can describe how I felt driving back to Gastonia. I wanted to talk to him again, but God said that I had to do things differently this time. I could not chase him. I had to allow him to pursue me. I had to wait for his eyes and ears to be opened before I could speak with him again. I did not know anything. I wanted him to invite me to church the next morning, but it did not happen. I wanted him to call me and say he had a wonderful time. I got nothing. I had to go through the night and the next day waiting, but I was ok with that. I was preparing to leave, and I had to pick up my son Taye because he was coming back with me to Georgia. The neighborhood he was in had poor cell service, so I left my phone in the car. When I returned to the car, I had missed his call. I called back, but his mom told me he just left to go back home. Maurice didn't have a phone at his place, so I had to wait until he would go back to his mom's house. The drive home, I was hoping he would return to his mom's and give me a call, but he didn't. It was all good. I got a call back, and that's all that matters at this point.

SO, YOU WANT TO MARRY ME?

On Monday, May 22, I was still on cloud nine. I had never been treated like that in all my life. Maurice was so kind and engaging, and I would love to get to know this person even if it was just as friends. I told my co-worker, Christy, about him, and she said he sounds like a winner. I agreed with her, but he had to come correct. I could not do it. It had to be all God. Later that day, I walked into the office and checked my phone. I had a missed call from him. I told her about it, and she said girl, go call him back. I called back, and he was just checking on me. Maurice said I had been on his mind since our meeting, and he wanted to talk to me. I told him that I got off at 5:30 and he could call me sometime after that. It was not long after getting off, he was ringing my phone. Wow! He was punctual and didn't have an excuse for why he could not talk. Maurice did not have a phone of his own, but he made a way to get in contact with me.

Our first conversation after the meeting, we talked for 5 hours non-stop. Maurice was so knowledgeable and full of wisdom. I could listen to him talk for hours and not feel overwhelmed. I learned so much about him in those five hours that I wanted to know more. I could not get enough. He was the breath of fresh air that I needed. Maurice was concerned with the things that concerned me. I did not have to fight to get a word in. He opened the floor for me and encouraged me to talk. I could not believe it. It was finally my time and my turn. We talked for the next couple of days, and things were getting better and better. I already loved him because of the love that God had filled my heart with. I could see myself with him and us going places together. I did not tell him that because he needed to see it without me hinting around about it. Wednesday, May 24th, I attended bible study with my friend, Amy, from work. We arrived early, and like clockwork, he called me. Maurice begins to say how his life had changed since meeting me. He used to have this reoccurring dream where he was lost and was afraid to enter that place, which was dark. Since our initial meeting, that dream had changed, and he had peace about going into the unknown. He has never had it again. I am sitting in the car taking it all in, and then he says, do you want a date? I was like, do I want a date. He said, not *do you want to go on a date*, but do you want a date to get married on? I said, are you saying that you want to marry me? He said yes. You pick a date, and I will see if I can hold up my end of it. I said no, I am not doing that. That is not my job. If you want to marry me, you will have to set the date. I am not playing games, and this is not how it's going down. You either know or you don't know. I can't help you with this one. You need to know for yourself. I understood the verbiage, but I could not make the decision. I spent a considerable part of my adulthood trying to convince men that I was the one. At this point, I know my worth, and you must be able to see it as well.

After that night, it did not hit me that I was on my way to getting married. I would watch a show called "Say Yes to the Dress," and I was in love with the dresses and fantasized about how my wedding would look. At this point, none of that mattered. Some things you must move into because it is time and prolonging it would not benefit you to satisfy your wants and people's expectation. The wedding wasn't the most important thing to me. Being able to walk with someone that God chose for you was at the top of my list. The big elaborate wedding was on the back burner. Doing the will of the Lord was at the forefront. He did not want a big wedding, and I did not either, so we agreed to get married at the courthouse. We knew we wanted to get married in our home state because we were both born in North Carolina. Our colors would be black and blue because black symbolizes death, and we were dying to ourselves to be raised to life in Christ. To this day, I am still in awe of the timing and the wisdom of God and how he puts things together.

We agreed upon the date of June 8th, 2017. The number 8 represents a new beginning, and this would be that for both of us. It was a Thursday, so it was not the norm, just like our meeting and our marriage. I told the kids, and they were happy for me if I was happy. They didn't have much to say because it was all happening so fast, but no one disagreed. His family was excited, but we did not make a public announcement. We felt like it was not necessary until after the nuptials, and if they were going to be happy for us, getting the news later would not change that love for us. It was in our hearts to proceed in the way we were going. I am still in shock, but grateful that the word spoke concerning my life was coming to pass right before my eyes.

I told my parents, and they seemed happy for me. My dad knew it had to be something for me to bring it to him. I did not introduce a lot of guys to my dad because deep down inside, I knew the relationship wasn't going anywhere. He said he needed to meet this man before he would give his official blessings. He immediately called him son, but he still had to ask him some questions. I agreed to travel up the road one last time before we got married, and we were scheduled to meet with my dad. It was my soon to be husband's birthday, so we went out to eat. He was so nervous that he could barely eat. The food wasn't all that great anyway but meeting someone's parents for the first time isn't a walk in the park, especially after knowing the person for only 2 weeks. I assured him that everything would be fine, and my dad would love you like I do. He already calls you son, so you are already in the family.

We left the restaurant and headed to my dad's. I'm not going to lie; I was becoming a bit nervous myself, but I had to hold it together because we both can't fall apart. He could be nervous, but I had to stand in my authority and confidence that this was the work of the Lord. We arrived, and not only is my dad and stepmom there, but his two sisters are there. I was like, "Lord, it just got real up in here." He has back up, and if they don't approve, I don't know what we're to do. We keep our composure, and he hits it off well with the family like I knew he would. He is the man for me, and they could see it just like I could. God did not disappoint, and I am so glad they are here to witness such greatness.

We leave from there, and I take him back to his place. It is late, and I really don't feel like driving back down the road. I thought I could stay the night with him, sleeping in separate rooms. Of course, it is a good idea, but it is not a God idea. My fiancé stops me dead in my tracks. He said I had to leave because not only was he protecting himself, but me as well. We did not want to put out the wrong image being that we were not married yet. Even though we know what we are doing, others looking on do not. He did not want to taint our testimony or our lives because we thought we could handle it. At first, I was upset, but I realized that is the way it's supposed to be done. Anybody else from my past would have allowed me to stay and just say we will repent afterward. He took charge of my soul to make sure when I tell this story, it will be from a place of truth and purity.

The next day I went with Maurice and his family to church and dinner. It was so amazing. Looking at some of his sisters and brothers and the love they have for one another was incredible. I felt right at home, and even one of his sister's children reminded me of my four. It was a day of thanksgiving and praise. I was marrying into an awesome family and had I not gone on my journey, none of this would be possible.

As I am preparing to leave his presence until Wednesday, it became harder to let go. I was so in love with him that I could not see my life without him. My stepmom advised me to make sure the courthouse does ceremonies on Thursday, so I called Monday to make sure. I found out that they do not conduct ceremonies on that day, and I had the privilege of asking my father to perform the ceremony. Of course, he agreed, and we would get married in his living room at 1 pm. Everything was falling into place, and I could not wait to become Mrs. Maurice Marcell Thornton. The next three days at work could not go by fast enough. My co-workers threw me a bridal shower the day before my wedding, and it was beautiful. They went above and beyond the call of duty. Everything they did was from the heart, and I am forever grateful for the love they showed towards me.

My fiancé had to come from South Carolina to get me because I did not have a car at the time, but he had already purposed in his heart to come and get us. He brought his nephew with him. Even though he got lost, the cellphone dies, and he didn't have anything concrete to go by, he made it to me. My heart lit up when he walked into the place. I could not believe that it was really happening. He had entered my life 18 days prior, and we were headed to the alter the next day. He was my knight in shining armor. Maurice was the gift that God had for me to receive. At the appointed time, he manifested, and here we are ready to become one. We hit the road, and we hit traffic. A four-hour drive took 7 hours to complete. It was an indication to me that my singleness had come to an end, and the next day I would be a married woman.

June 8th, 2017 began just like any other day except this time, I would end the day a married woman. My daughter is with me as we get up to go meet him at the Gaston County Courthouse to get our marriage license. Maurice gets lost, and I leave to go and get him. I am not nervous at all because no matter what happens, he keeps showing up. So many things could have stopped him from proceeding, but his yes to God meant more. We get our license, and they head to get something to eat. I go to my friend Jackie's house to get ready. I did not have anything new because I left my shoes in Georgia. I borrowed her shoes, and even though we wear different sizes, they were a perfect fit. I do my hair, and it is getting closer to time for me to head to my dad's. Jackie comes with me as a witness, and her support had gotten me through some rough patches, but here, we are together. I can't thank her enough for being there with me on one of the most important days of my life. I get to my dad's, and he is already there waiting. I walk in, and they rush me to the back room. I am thinking we are going to just meet up, go in the living room and say our vows, and that would be it. I didn't know my day had arranged the living room in such a way that it resembled something out of a fairy tale. As I am waiting, I am sitting in the back, reflecting on all that has happened. Here I am back at my dad's house, but this time I am leaving a married woman. God told me that when I left his house, I would be married. He did not say when, but I held on to those words and look at me now.

The walk down the hallway to the living room was magical. My brother Christopher was playing the guitar, which I had no idea he would do. When I turn the corner, I see my children, my two aunts, his mother and nephew, my cousin, and the room is decorated in all white. My dad went all out for my special day, and it was the most beautiful room I had ever seen. It made me feel like he took my day seriously, and he wanted me to have the best. I see my fiancé standing waiting on me. No longer did I have to wait on him to show up. He was now waiting for me to meet him at the altar. That moment brought tears to my eyes, and the joy that filled my heart has never left even up until this day.

My dad does the ceremony, and we have written our own vows. This day could not have been any better because it was already perfect. Years ago, I had written a wedding song for someone else. Little did I know that I would end up singing it at my own wedding. Sometimes we do things for one reason, but you end up using it later down the line. When I finished, I looked at my dad, and he was wiping the tears away. I knew then that he was pleased with what had taken place on that day in his home. He introduces us as husband and wife, and we exit the room as a married couple.

WHAT I LEARNED

I don't know what was more exciting about that day, getting married or being in the company of those that love you for who you are. The expectations that were put on my life to produce had been thrown out the window, and I was finally free to be me. The marriage was the beginning of my new life in God. The last thing on our list became the first thing on God's. It is the foundation that our legacy will be built upon. The process of getting my life together was more than I could have ever imagined. Nobody sees the behind the scene things that you must push through. Going after what is yours can upset those that are around you. It can make them nervous for you, but you can't let that stop you. What God has for you is for you, and no matter how they feel about it, it is your life to live. God is the clock, and when your hour comes, you must be ready to move in it no matter what is going on around you. If you wait for the circumstance to be perfect, you will never make a move. You will always be in a place you say you want to break free from. You must take a chance even if you can't or don't understand the reason behind it. God will never lead you astray, and you can always count on him to show up right on time.

He knows the plans he has for you, and when you start putting your earthly understanding on a heavenly concept, you will be confused and feeling like giving up. But when you keep your mind on things above and the ability of the great I am, you will see things you have never seen done in your family or generation. You only must believe. He doesn't need anything but your faith. He isn't asking your family, friends, coworkers, church members, etc. to have the faith that your circumstance will work for the good. He is talking to you, showing you and giving you the information you need to receive from him. No one can stop you, but you. Don't let your past talk to you about your future. It has nothing good to say about it. Let your past die so your future can live.

ACKNOWLEDGMENTS

It's been said that it takes a village to raise a child. I have found that statement to be true. When I decided to write this book, I knew I would need help. I could not do this on my own. God placed some wonderful people along my path. I thank God for my village, and without them, this would not be possible. I am forever grateful for their selfless acts of kindness and love, shown towards me.

Chase and Abby Bowles
Diane Wright
Sarita Jackson
Wendy Cunningham
Amy Carter
Allyson Holmes
Kim Holmes
Matthew Shepard

Brenda McCormick
Katrina Sharman
Sarah Hawkins
Lilli Tucker
Kacie Scoggins
Ashley Dean
Jodi Meza
Al and Heather Davis
Pastor Robbins Young
James and Nancy Young
Vanessa Dean
Ellen Brookshire
Kristi Elkins
William and Mary Bennett
Rachelle Johnson
Gladies Owens
LaGrethia Kindred
Bishop Alonzo Rodgers
Thomas and Allison Brown
Shawn Tate
Jason and Tabitha Blair
Diane Johnson
Ben Corbin

www.ingramcontent.com/pod-product-compliance
Lightning Source LLC
Chambersburg PA
CBHW021959290426
44108CB00012B/1137